PRACTICAL GOURMET™
Good Friends, Great Grilling

Pictured on front cover:
Mango Teriyaki-Glazed Turkey,
page 148

Practical Gourmet
Copyright © Company's Coming Publishing Limited

First Printing March 2009
Library and Archives Canada Cataloguing in Publication
Good friends, great grilling.
(Practical gourmet)
Includes index.
At head of title: Company's Coming.
ISBN 978-1-897069-91-2
1. Barbecue cookery. I. Series.
TX840.B3G66 2009   641.5'784   C2008-904013-9

Published by
Company's Coming Publishing Limited
2311 – 96 Street
Edmonton, Alberta, Canada T6N 1G3
Tel: 780-450-6223   Fax: 780-450-1857
www.companyscoming.com

Company's Coming is a registered trademark owned by
Company's Coming Publishing Limited

Printed in China

We acknowledge the financial support of the Government of Canada through the Book Publishing Industry Development Program (BPIDP) for our publishing activities.

Nutrition Information Guidelines

Each recipe has been analyzed using the Canadian Nutrient File from Health Canada, which is based upon the United States Department of Agriculture (USDA) Nutrient Database.
- If more than one ingredient is listed, such as butter (or hard margarine), or if a range is given (1 - 2 tsp., 5 - 10 mL), only the first ingredient or first amount is analyzed.
- The lesser number of servings is used if a range is stated.
- Ingredients indicating "sprinkle," "optional" or "for garnish" are not included in the nutrition information.
- Milk used is 1% M.F. (milk fat), unless otherwise noted.

Vera Mazurak, Ph.D (Nutritionist)

Acknowledgements

Good Friends, Great Grilling *was created through the dedicated efforts of the people listed below:*

Editor-in-Chief	Eleana Yun
Research and Development Manager	Jill Corbett
Editorial Director	Tabea Berg
Editor	Sandra Bit
Recipe Editor	Janet Fowler
Senior Food Editor	Lynda Elsenheimer
Food Editor	Mary Anne Korn
Researcher	Frieda Lovig
Senior Recipe Tester	James Bullock
Recipe Testers	Allison Dosman
	Audrey Smetaniuk
Copy Editor/Proofreader	Laurie Penner
Contributors	Rita Feutl
	Amy Hough
	Rebecca Kostiuk
	Patricia Meili-Bullock
	Laurie Stempfle
Creative Director	Heather Markham
Design and Production	Titania Lam
Photography	Stephe Tate Photo
Photo Assistant	Heather Latimer
Food Stylist	Ashley Billey
Prop Stylist	Snez Ferenac
Prep Assistant	Linda Dobos
Production Supervisor	Matt Bromley
Nutritionist	Vera Mazurak, Ph.D
Founding Author	Jean Paré
President	Grant Lovig
Vice President, Production and Creative	Alanna Wilson

Our special thanks to the following businesses for providing numerous props for photography:

Anchor Hocking Canada
Danesco Inc.
Pier 1 Imports®
Stokes
Wal-Mart Canada Inc.
Pfaltzgraff Canada
Cherison Enterprises Inc.
Canhome Global

Casa Bugatti
Wiltshire®
Totally Bamboo
Klass Works
Out of the Fire Studio
Michaels The Art And Crafts Store
Winners Stores

We gratefully acknowledge the following suppliers for their generous support of our Test and Photography kitchens:

Broil King Barbecues
Corelle®
Hamilton Beach® Canada

Lagostina®
Proctor Silex® Canada
Tupperware®

Contents

Smouldering Starters 12
Flame-kissed appetizers

• Spiced Lime Shrimp With Chilled Avocado Soup • Paneer Vegetable Kabobs With Mint "Raita" • Margarita Chicken Cocktails • Puffed Pizza Margherita • Tuscan Turkey Rolls • Antipasto Kabobs • Bourbon Chicken Wings • Tapenade-Stuffed Pork • Shrimp And Pineapple Citrus Skewers

Heat It Up, Cool It Down 32
Show-stopping meal salads

• Lemon Grass Beef Salad • Grilled Chicken And Squash On Spinach Salad • Lobster, Fennel And Pear Salad • Romano Ciabatta Vegetable Salad • Farmers' Market Pork Tenderloin Salad • Tandoori Paneer Salad

Breadwinners 46
Innovative burgers, dogs and sandwiches

• Chipotle Chicken Burgers With Avocado Mayonnaise • Drunken Lamb Burgers With Cranberry Dijon Mustard • Sassy Stuffed Portobello Burgers • Lemon Grass Crab Cakes With Pencil Asparagus • Greek Pita Burgers • Curry Salmon Burgers With Mango Chutney Mayo • Blue Cheese Beer Burgers • Smoked Turkey Quesadillas With Salsa Guacamole • Spicy Asian Patties With Pear Salsa • Mediterranean Veggie Focaccia • Tuna Squares With Wasabi Ginger Slaw • Brown Rice Veggie Patties With Tomato Relish • Out-Of-The-Park Jalapeño Dawgs • Herbed Turkey Burgers With Fresh Tomato Ketchup

Spike & Ignite 76
Sizzling skewers

• Souvlaki Skewers • Chicken Tikka Kabobs • Crab-Stuffed Pepper Skewers • Jerk Pork Rolls • Moroccan Fish Skewers With Lemon Beet Coulis • Apple Brandy Bratwurst Bites • Cajun Chicken Wings • Sesame Scallops With Maple Cream • Saltimbocca Skewers With Arugula Salad • Quince-Glazed Chicken Skewers

Fire & Water 97
Fish and seafood with flare

• Rosemary-Skewered Seafood • Bourbon Pepper-Crusted Salmon • Scallop Skewers With Black Bean Avocado Relish • Pineapple-Planked Prawns • Smoked Fennel Trout • Grilled Red Snapper With Lime Butter • Herbed Bulgur-Stuffed Calamari • Maple Walnut Arctic Char • Woven Salmon And Halibut With Tahini Tartar Sauce • Jerk Bass Fillets • Seared Tuna Steak With Sesame Ginger Sauce • Mussels In Spicy Coconut Broth • Lemon Ginger Halibut • Cherry-Glazed Salmon

Birds Of A Feather 128
Pleasing poultry that gets away from the everyday

• Chai-Smoked Chicken • Pomegranate Chili Chicken • Thai Turkey Steaks • Buttery Spiced Chicken • Twist Of Lime Chicken With Three-Tomato Salsa • Wine "Poached" Chicken With Rosemary Garlic Vegetables • Cinnamon Cherry Duck Breasts • Coconut Pesto-Stuffed Chicken Breasts • Chicken Churrasco • Mango Teriyaki-Glazed Turkey • Grilled Curry Quail With Lime Mangoes • Sweet Spice Chicken With Smoky Rhubarb Barbecue Sauce • Hoisin Five-Spice Drumsticks • Brined Turkey With Orange Thyme Sauce • Greek Chicken Thighs

Cuts Meet Coals 160
Steaks, chops and ribs—artfully prepared to perfection

• Cumin Pork Chops With Corn Salsa • Runaway Five-Spice Ribs • Herb And Pepper Steak • Lamb Chops With Hazelnut Gremolata • Chili Cherry Beef Ribs Pork Noisette • Orange Chili-Stuffed Pork Chops • Tropical T-Bone Steaks With Papaya Relish • Curry Coconut Ribs • Grilled Butterflied Lamb With Pomegranate Reduction • Mole-Ole! Steak With Chili Salsa • Prosciutto Pork Mignon With Parsley Cilantro Crema • Bourbon Street Steak With Citrus Butter • Miso-Glazed Pork Chops With Wasabi Mayonnaise • Jamaican Flank Steak • Moroccan Lamb Shanks • Filet Mignon With Asparagus And Smoked Salmon

Taking It Slow 196
Tender roasts and showcase meats

• Porcini-Rubbed Beef Roast • Meatloaf With Chipotle Ketchup • Raspberry Balsamic Cornish Hens • Cocoa-Crusted Tenderloin With Stilton Crumble • Lemon Pistachio Pork • Rosemary Plum Leg Of Lamb • Port-Glazed Pork Tenderloin With Stilton Pears • Dijon Prime Rib

Jean Paré grew up with an understanding that family, friends and home cooking are the key ingredients for a good life. A busy mother of four, Jean developed a knack for creating quick and easy recipes using everyday ingredients. For 18 years, she operated a successful catering business from her home kitchen in the small prairie town of Vermilion, Alberta, Canada. During that time, she earned a reputation for great food, courteous service and reasonable prices. Steadily increasing demand for her recipes led to the founding of Company's Coming Publishing Limited in 1981.

The first Company's Coming cookbook, *150 Delicious Squares*, was an immediate bestseller. As more titles were introduced, the company quickly earned the distinction of publishing Canada's most popular cookbooks. Company's Coming continues to gain new supporters in Canada, the United States and throughout the world by adhering to Jean's Golden Rule of Cooking: *Never share a recipe you wouldn't use yourself*. It's an approach that has worked—millions of times over!

A familiar and trusted name in the kitchen, Company's Coming has extended its reach throughout the home with other types of books and products for everyday living.

Though humble about her achievements, Jean Paré is one of North America's most loved and recognized authors. The recipient of many awards, Jean was appointed Member of the Order of Canada, her country's highest lifetime achievement honour.

Today, Jean Paré's influence as founding author, mentor and moral compass is evident in all aspects of the company she founded. Every recipe created and every product produced upholds the family values and work ethic she instilled. Readers the world over will continue to be encouraged and inspired by her legacy for generations to come.

Foreword

Good company and great food create a powerful combination. When laughter and conversation mix with the heady fragrance and flavours of delicious fare, we are not just sharing a meal—we are nourishing our lives. Artfully prepared dishes awaken the senses and please the palate. And here's the secret: It can be simple!

Casual, fun and delicious—this is the essence of backyard grilling. When the warmth of summer beckons us outside, the last thing we want to do is cook dinner indoors. Grilling takes us not just outside of our kitchens, but beyond the formality of the dining room and into a space where long summer nights encourage us to enjoy the good life with friends and family. And the good life was never so appetizing, or so easy! The flavourful marinades, rubs and infusions in this book make playing with food a grownup affair, while easy cleanup, minimal planning and quick results make grilling especially appealing.

Like *Small Plates for Sharing*, the first title in the Practical Gourmet series, *Good Friends, Great Grilling* is designed to help home cooks create sumptuous food without the fuss. It features full-colour photographs of each recipe, preparation tips and tricks, how-to photos, imaginative presentation ideas and helpful information on entertaining, so you and your guests can really savour the food—and your time together.

Good Friends, Great Grilling opens the door to the backyard and invites you to experience the thrill of the grill. The focus is on the unique flavours and flexibility of grilled food, and the way that cooking on the deck or patio makes for outdoor entertaining at its best. Using seasonal and locally available meats and produce, home chefs can don their aprons and heat things up—in the lazy days of summer and all year long.

Experiment with the 93 sophisticated but approachable recipes in this book; then treat guests to your favourites. Pull out your patio lanterns and create the perfect atmosphere for connecting with close friends. After all, good friends deserve great grilling!

Great Grilling Basics

The recipes in this book use a number of grilling tools and methods. To ensure fabulous results, familiarize (or reacquaint) yourself with some basic grilling techniques, tips and tools.

GENERAL TIPS FOR SUCCESS

- Prepare the grill:
  - Make sure the grill is clean to start with.
  - Preheat the barbecue. Use a barbecue thermometer to get an accurate reading on the inside to establish and then maintain the right temperature. This becomes especially important for indirect grilling.
  - Grease the grill well to prevent food from sticking.
- Unless otherwise directed, keep the lid closed at all times. This helps maintain the temperature of the barbecue, reduces risk of flare-ups and reduces cooking time.
- Watch the weather. The temperature outdoors will affect the barbecue's internal temperature. Account for this in cooking times.
- Don't leave the barbecue unattended, especially if there are children nearby.
- Use a meat thermometer to determine meat's doneness. To get an accurate reading, insert the thermometer into the thickest part of the meat.
- When using marinades, always let food marinate in the refrigerator. If you want to use the leftover marinade, always boil it gently for at least five minutes first.

BASIC METHODS

DIRECT GRILLING

This is what most people think of when they think of grilling. Used mainly for small or thin cuts of meat, direct grilling is simply that—cooking the food over the flame or heat source.

Getting ready

For a non-gas barbecue, light coals in a chimney starter and allow them to heat until they begin to turn red. Carefully dump them into the bottom of the barbecue, spreading them in an even layer. For a gas barbecue, simply light the burner or burners over which the food will be cooked.

Barbecue temperatures

For the recipes in *Good Friends, Great Grilling*, we've referred to levels of heat—low, medium-low, medium, medium-high and high. The following table shows the temperature ranges that correspond with each level of heat:

Level	Barbecue's Internal Temperature
Low	300°F – 350°F (150°C – 175°C)
Medium-low	350°F – 400°F (175°C – 205°C)
Medium	400°F – 450°F (205°C – 230°C)
Medium-high	450°F – 500°F (230°C – 260°C)
High	500°F+ (260°C+)

INDIRECT GRILLING

When you are using your barbecue the same way you would an indoor oven, you're using the indirect grilling method. This method is usually used to cook anything that requires a longer cooking time, such as ribs or roasts. To grill indirectly, place food in the barbecue on a rotisserie, on a rack above the grill or on top of an unlit burner. Indirect cooking's more moderate heat and longer cooking time are also perfect for smoking meat.

Getting ready

For a non-gas barbecue, light coals in a chimney starter and allow them to heat until they begin to turn red. Carefully dump the coals in the portion of the barbecue that will be away from the food you're cooking, either on one side or on two opposite sides. For a gas barbecue, simply light the burner or burners, but cook the food over the burner or burners that are not lit.

Barbecue temperatures

As with direct grilling, we've referred to levels of heat—medium-low, medium and high. The following table shows the temperature ranges that correspond with each level of heat:

Level	Barbecue's Internal Temperature
Medium-low	250°F – 325°F (120°C – 160°C)
Medium	350°F – 400°F (175°C – 205°C)
High	425°F+ (220°C+)

More indirect grilling methods

These methods allow for a lot of variation in how you prepare your food. In *Good Friends, Great Grilling*, we've experimented with the following indirect grilling methods:

- Rotisserie grilling – This method uses a spit that rotates in the barbecue to allow for slow, even cooking. Be sure to follow the manufacturer's instructions for your particular barbecue rotisserie.
- Smoking – This is a process that infuses the meat with smoky flavours while it is being grilled. Depending on the type of wood chips being used, the meat will pick up different flavour notes from the smoke produced. To smoke meat, place a smoker box filled with pre-soaked wood chips on one burner and turn it on to High. Once smoke begins to form, adjust the burner temperature to achieve the desired internal barbecue temperature. Cook your meat over the unlit burner, according to your recipe. To make your own smoker box, add soaked and drained wood chips to a 7 x 3 inch (18 x 7.5 cm) disposable foil pan. Cover tightly with foil. Poke a few holes in the foil to allow smoke to escape.

Using a drip pan

A drip pan placed underneath indirectly grilled meat will catch any grease or meat juices released while the meat is cooking. To use a drip pan, place it on one burner and light the opposite burner. Place your food on the grill rack that sits over the drip pan.

Nothing beats a smooth, ice-cold brew to go with something hot off the grill. Choose the best beer for your menu with these cool tips.

Pale Ales

- Medium-bodied pale ales balance the flavours of hops and barley. India pale ales tend to be slightly more bitter than regular pale ales. Ales generally have a stronger flavour than traditional beers.

- Pale ales complement lamb, beef roasts and steaks. These beers also go well with rich-tasting poultry, such as turkey and duck. Because they highlight intense flavours, pale ales make a great pairing for spicy dishes.

Lambic beers

- Lambic beers are made from a combination of wheat and malted barley. Fruit is sometimes added during aging. Lambic beers are aged in casks and can be slightly sour when aged for a shorter period, while those varieties that are aged for longer periods tend to be more mellow.

- Because of their fruity flavours, these beers are great alongside fresh fruit dishes. Lambic beers also complement soft-ripened cheeses like brie.

Brown and Amber Ales

- Brown ales are full-bodied, slightly sweet and lightly hopped. The colour is a darker brown or amber colour due to the caramelized malts used to produce these ales. Scotch ale, another form of brown ale, has a strong, malty flavour.

- Brown and amber ales pair with hearty, flavourful foods like Mexican dishes, hamburgers and pizza. Brown ales can also be served with green salads. Amber ales do not make a good match for sweeter foods, because of their malty flavour.

Porters and Stouts

- Porters and stouts are usually heavy, dark and strongly flavoured beers that include roasted malt, which accounts for their dark colour and strong flavour. Most porters have a balanced flavour, both slightly bitter and sweet. Stouts and porters tend to be higher in alcohol content than other varieties of beer.

- The more intense flavours of porters and stouts balance strongly flavoured foods like oysters, smoked cheeses and meat dishes that include brown gravies. Sweeter varieties of stout can also be served with rich, chocolatey desserts.

Lagers and Pilsners

- Lagers tend to be light and bubbly with a golden colour. Pilsners are a light, pale variety of lager—generally with milder flavours and a slightly hoppy taste.

- Lagers' lighter flavours make them a great complement to mild-tasting foods like chicken, fish and green salads. Lagers also work great with fried foods and spicy Asian dishes because of their refreshing qualities.

Bocks

- Though traditionally a German beer, many American varieties of bocks are now available. Bocks tend to be dark and bitter, but they are balanced with some sweetness. Bocks are full-bodied and have a malty flavour.

- Bocks complement hearty grilled fare, including sausages and marinated meats. The strong flavours in bock beers can cut through—and balance out—spicier dishes.

Sometimes the opening act steals the show. Fire up the barbecue and fire up the flavour with morsels that captivate the senses. Recipes like Spiced Lime Shrimp With Chilled Avocado Soup and Tuscan Turkey Rolls are a fitting way to launch your patio party or backyard soiree.

Smouldering Starters

Flame-kissed appetizers

Spiced Lime Shrimp
With Chilled Avocado Soup

Large avocado, chilled, chopped	1	1
Prepared chicken broth, chilled	1/2 cup	125 mL
Lemon juice	2 tbsp.	30 mL
Granulated sugar	1 tsp.	5 mL
Ground cumin	1 tsp.	5 mL
Salt	1/4 tsp.	1 mL
Whipping cream	1/2 cup	125 mL
Brown sugar, packed	2 tbsp.	30 mL
Tequila	2 tsp.	10 mL
Chili powder	1 tsp.	5 mL
Salt	1/2 tsp.	2 mL
Uncooked large shrimp (peeled and deveined), butterflied	1 lb.	454 g
Lime juice	1 tbsp.	15 mL

In a blender or food processor, process first 6 ingredients until smooth. Add cream and process until just combined. Pour into 8 small cups or bowls.

Combine next 4 ingredients. Add shrimp and stir. Cook in greased preheated barbecue wok on direct medium-high heat for about 3 minutes, stirring occasionally, until shrimp turn pink.

Add lime juice and toss. Serve with soup. Serves 8.

1 serving: 172 Calories; 10.1 g Total Fat (4.2 g Mono, 1.1 g Poly, 4.0 g Sat); 105 mg Cholesterol; 8 g Carbohydrate; 2 g Fibre; 13 g Protein; 408 mg Sodium

---

GARNISH
lime wedges

TIP
Make this recipe with any size shrimp you happen to have on hand. Adjust cooking times to ensure they are served up tender and juicy.

PRESENTATION SUGGESTION
Serve the soup in small cups or glasses on interesting plates. Nestle the shrimp alongside.

Lime-finished shrimp and creamy avocado soup
perform in a **duet of flavours**—enjoy them together
to fully appreciate the **complex blend of seasonings.**

Invite good friends to share **comfort food** with Southwest flair. Smoked **jalapeño** peppers add a **fiery twist** to the ketchup for everyone's favourite meatloaf, making the possibility of leftovers nonexistent.

Raspberry Balsamic Cornish Hens

Butter, softened	1/4 cup	60 mL
Italian seasoning	2 tbsp.	30 mL
Grated lemon zest	2 tsp.	10 cm
Salt	1 tsp.	5 cm
Cornish hens (about 1 1/2 lbs., 680 g, each)	2	2
Seedless raspberry jam	1/2 cup	125 mL
Balsamic vinegar	1/4 cup	60 mL
Lemon juice	1 tbsp.	15 mL

Combine first 4 ingredients.

Carefully loosen skin on hens, but do not remove. Stuff butter mixture between skin and meat, spreading mixture as evenly as possible (see Tip, below). Chill, covered, for 30 minutes.

Combine remaining 3 ingredients in a saucepan. Gently boil on medium until thickened. Prepare grill for indirect medium heat with a drip pan. Cook hens, breast-side down, for 20 minutes. Turn. Cook for 30 to 40 minutes, brushing occasionally with jam mixture, until meat thermometer inserted in thickest part of breast reaches 180°F (82°C). Cover with foil and let stand for 10 minutes. Cut hens in half to serve. Serves 4.

1 serving: 617 Calories; 39.7 g Total Fat (15.4 g Mono, 6.0 g Poly, 15.0 g Sat); 234 mg Cholesterol; 29 g Carbohydrate; trace Fibre; 35 g Protein; 770 mg Sodium

GARNISH
sprigs of basil
fresh raspberries

TIP
Inserting the butter between the meat and the skin will help keep the hens moist and flavourful.

Stuffed with **lemon zest** and Italian seasonings and basted with a **raspberry-balsamic** sauce, these small birds boast enormous flavour.

Cocoa-Crusted Tenderloin
With Stilton Crumble

Beef tenderloin roast	2 1/2 lbs.	1.1 kg
Olive oil	2 tbsp.	30 mL
Brown sugar, packed	2 tbsp.	30 mL
Coarsely ground pepper	2 tbsp.	30 mL
Cocoa, sifted if lumpy	2 tbsp.	30 mL
Smoked sweet paprika	2 tbsp.	30 mL
Salt	1 1/4 tsp.	6 mL
Stilton cheese, crumbled	2 oz.	57 g

Rub entire surface of roast with olive oil. Combine next 5 ingredients and rub over roast. Prepare grill for indirect medium-high heat with a drip pan. Cook for 30 minutes, then rotate roast 180°. Cook for about 30 minutes until internal temperature reaches 145°F (63°C) for medium-rare or until roast reaches desired doneness. Cover with foil and let stand for 15 minutes. Cut roast into 1/2 inch (12 mm) thick slices.

Sprinkle with cheese. Serves 8.

1 serving: 240 Calories; 13.7 g Total Fat (5.7 g Mono, 0.7 g Poly, 4.9 g Sat); 59 mg Cholesterol; 5 g Carbohydrate; 1 g Fibre; 24 g Protein; 512 mg Sodium

TIP
If you can, get a tenderloin roast cut from the centre of the loin for an even-shaped roast.

ABOUT PAPRIKA
A spice most closely associated with Hungary and Hungarian cuisine (think chicken paprikash), paprika is also used extensively to flavour and colour Spanish, Portuguese, Turkish and Indian dishes. Paprika is divided into several categories depending on level of spiciness and colour, but the most common variety is derived from dried sweet red peppers and is known as sweet paprika.

An **elegant** entree seasoned with a touch of the unpredictable—**cocoa and stilton**—this tenderloin demands fine china and **candlelight** at any time of year. Match this with your favourite full-bodied **red wine**.

Lemon Pistachio Pork

Liquid honey	1/3 cup	75 mL
Lemon juice	3 tbsp.	50 mL
Finely grated ginger root	1 tbsp.	15 mL
Grated lemon zest (see Tip, page 124)	2 tsp.	10 mL
Ground cinnamon	1/2 tsp.	2 mL
Coarsely chopped roasted pistachios	1 cup	250 mL
Fine dry bread crumbs	1 cup	250 mL
Dark raisins	1/3 cup	75 mL
Dried cranberries	1/3 cup	75 mL
Boneless pork rib roast, frozen for 30 minutes (see Why To, below)	2 – 3 lbs.	900 g – 1.4 kg
Olive oil	2 tsp.	10 mL
Coarsely ground pepper	3 tbsp.	50 mL
Smoked sweet paprika	1 tbsp.	15 mL
Seasoned salt	1 1/2 tsp.	7 mL

Combine first 5 ingredients.

Add next 4 ingredients and stir until combined.

Place roast, fat-side up, on a cutting board. Using a sharp knife, cut horizontally, about 1/2 inch (12 mm) from bottom, almost, but not quite, through to other side (see Why To, below). Open roast like a book and cut through thicker half of roast, about 1/2 inch (12 mm) from bottom, almost, but not quite, through to other side. Repeat, if necessary, until roast is an even 1/2 inch (12 mm) thickness. Spread pistachio mixture over roast, leaving a 1/2 inch (12 mm) border. Roll up tightly from short edge to enclose. Tie with butcher's string at 1 inch (2.5 cm) intervals (see How To, page 28).

Brush entire surface of roast with olive oil. Combine remaining 3 ingredients and sprinkle over roast. Prepare grill for indirect medium heat with a drip pan. Cook roast, fat-side up, for about 1 1/2 hours, turning once, until internal temperature of pork reaches at least 140°F (60°C) or until desired doneness. Cover with foil and let stand for 15 minutes. Remove string and cut into 1/2 inch (12 mm) thick slices. Serves 8.

1 serving: 417 Calories; 16.6 g Total Fat (8.4 g Mono, 3.3 g Poly, 3.8 g Sat); 62 mg Cholesterol; 38 g Carbohydrate; 3 g Fibre; 30 g Protein; 434 mg Sodium

HOW TO CUT ROAST

GARNISH
lemon wedges
dried cranberries
pistachios

WHY TO
Partially freezing the roast
will help it retain its shape
while cutting.

Crusted with pepper and stuffed with a sweet dried fruit and pistachio filling, this roast needs little attention once it's on the grill, leaving you free to spoil yourself with some down time before the guests arrive.

Rosemary Plum Leg Of Lamb

Cans of prune plums, drained and pitted (14 oz., 398 mL, each)	3	3
Plum jam	1/2 cup	125 mL
Balsamic vinegar	2 tbsp.	30 mL
Brown sugar, packed	2 tbsp.	30 mL
Fresh rosemary, chopped	2 tbsp.	30 mL
Finely grated ginger root	1 tbsp.	15 mL
Ground cinnamon	1 1/2 tsp.	7 mL
Salt	1/2 tsp.	2 mL
Ground cardamom	1/4 tsp.	1 mL
Ground cloves	1/8 tsp.	0.5 mL
Boneless leg of lamb roast	3 1/2 – 4 lbs.	1.6 – 1.8 kg

In a blender or food processor, process first 10 ingredients until smooth. Reserve 2 cups (500 mL).

Prepare grill for indirect medium heat with a drip pan. Cook roast for 1 hour. Turn and cook for about 1 hour, brushing often with plum sauce, until internal temperature reaches 145°F (63°C) for medium-rare or until roast reaches desired doneness. Cover with foil and let stand for 15 minutes. Cut roast into slices. Warm reserved plum sauce and serve with roast. Serves 10.

1 serving: 425 Calories; 14.8 g Total Fat (6.3 g Mono, 1.1 g Poly, 6.0 g Sat); 106 mg Cholesterol; 42 g Carbohydrate; 2 g Fibre; 32 g Protein; 218 mg Sodium

---

GARNISH
sprigs of rosemary
plum wedges

TIP
Ask your butcher to completely de-bone, tie and trim the lamb roast for you.

ABOUT LAMB
If butchered before it's a year old, sheep meat is called lamb. After, it's known as mutton and has a stronger flavour.

Exotic spices and luscious summer plums meld as the lamb roasts slowly on the grill. The aromas will entice neighbours to appear at your gate bearing bottles of shiraz.

Port-Glazed Pork Tenderloin
With Stilton Pears

Redcurrant jelly	1/2 cup	125 mL
Ruby port	1/2 cup	125 mL
Ground ginger	1/2 tsp.	2 mL
Salt	1/2 tsp.	2 mL
Pepper	1/2 tsp.	2 mL
Ground cloves	1/8 tsp.	0.5 mL
Pork tenderloin, trimmed of fat	1 lb.	454 g
Salt, sprinkle		
Pepper, sprinkle		
Firm medium unpeeled pears, cored and halved	2	2
Cooking oil	1 tsp.	5 mL
Stilton cheese	4 oz.	113 g

Combine first 6 ingredients in a saucepan. Gently boil on medium, stirring occasionally, until reduced and thickened. Remove from heat and let stand until cool. Reserve 1/4 cup (60 mL).

Sprinkle tenderloin with salt and pepper. Grill on direct medium-high heat for about 25 minutes, turning often and brushing with reserved glaze during final 5 minutes of cooking, until internal temperature reaches 160°F (71°C). Cover with foil and let stand for 5 minutes. Cut diagonally into 12 slices.

Brush cut-sides of pears with cooking oil. Grill pears, cut-side down, on direct medium-high heat for about 4 minutes. Rotate pears 45° after 2 minutes to create attractive grill marks. Turn pears cut-side up and top with cheese. Cook for about 2 minutes until cheese is softened. Serve with tenderloin and remaining glaze. Serves 4.

1 serving: 455 Calories; 14.6 g Total Fat (2.8 g Mono, 0.9 g Poly, 6.8 g Sat); 97 mg Cholesterol; 43 g Carbohydrate; 2 g Fibre; 31 g Protein; 738 mg Sodium

GARNISH
fresh chopped chives

ABOUT STILTON
Although another blue cheese may be substituted for Stilton, its buttery quality goes particularly well with both pears and port.

TIP
Pork tenderloin is low in fat and small in size, so it can be cooked quickly. It is a good meat for grilling for this reason. Because it has little fat, it is not as robustly flavoured as some other cuts of pork, so it goes well with stronger-tasting ingredients for more depth of flavour.

The tantalizing choice is yours: green-skinned pears pair well visually with the fresh chives, while red-skinned pears play off the redcurrant jelly and ruby port. Either way, the result is fabulous!

Dijon Prime Rib

Bone-in prime rib roast (see Tip, below)	6 lbs.	2.7 kg
Garlic cloves, halved lengthwise	4	4
Dijon mustard (with whole seeds)	1/3 cup	75 mL
Mayonnaise	3 tbsp.	50 mL
Prepared horseradish	2 tbsp.	30 mL
Liquid honey	1 tsp.	5 mL
Salt	1 tsp.	5 mL
Coarsely ground pepper	1 tsp.	5 mL

Cut 8 slits randomly in roast with a small, sharp knife. Push garlic clove halves halfway into each slit.

Combine remaining 6 ingredients. Spoon over roast, spreading evenly over top and sides. Prepare grill for indirect medium heat with a drip pan. Cook, bone-side down, for 1 hour, then rotate roast 180°. Cook for about 1 1/2 hours until internal temperature reaches 145°F (63°C) for medium-rare or until roast reaches desired doneness. Cover with foil and let stand for 15 minutes (see Why To, below). Cut roast into slices. Serves 12.

1 serving: *598 Calories; 50.9 g Total Fat (22.4 g Mono, 2.3 g Poly, 20.4 g Sat); 118 mg Cholesterol; 2 g Carbohydrate; trace Fibre; 31 g Protein; 403 mg Sodium*

WHY TO
Be sure to let roasts rest for 15 to 30 minutes after coming off the barbecue (the bigger the roast, the longer the stand time). Letting it stand will give the meat a chance to finish cooking (it will come up several degrees) and the juices will be reabsorbed into the meat, making your roast more moist and succulent.

TIP
When you purchase the roast, have the butcher cut off the ribs then tie them back in place. While the meat is roasting, it will take on the delicious flavour of the bones, but they can be removed easily from the roast just before carving.

For decadence, few things match a **prime rib**. The barbecue not only adds a distinctive smokiness to the roast, but the **garlic cloves** roast while cooking, infusing the meat with **fabulous** flavour.

Side By Side

Select any of these sides, alone or in combination, as an accompaniment to your grilling showpiece.

FLAVOUR ACCENTS

Great with any grilled meats or vegetables. (To make butter logs for slicing, see How To, page 186.)

- **Blue Cheese Butter:** Combine 1/4 cup (60 mL) softened butter with 2 tbsp. (30 mL) crumbled Stilton and 1/2 tsp. (2 mL) pepper.
- **Chipotle Butter:** Combine 1/4 cup (60 mL) softened butter with 1 tsp. (5 mL) finely chopped chipotle pepper in adobo sauce.
- **Curry Butter:** Combine 2 tbsp. (30 mL) softened butter, 2 tbsp. (30 mL) olive oil, 2 tsp. (10 mL) hot curry paste and 1 tsp. (5 mL) liquid honey.
- **Peppercorn Rosemary Butter:** Combine 1/4 cup (60 mL) softened butter with 1/2 tsp. (2 mL) crushed black peppercorns and 2 tsp. (10 mL) chopped fresh rosemary.
- **Smoked Paprika Butter:** Combine 1/4 cup (60 mL) softened butter with 2 tsp. (10 mL) smoked sweet paprika.
- **Smoky Cranberry Butter:** Combine 1/4 cup (60 mL) softened butter with 2 tbsp. (30 mL) jellied cranberry sauce and 2 tsp. (10 mL) smoky barbecue sauce.

BREAD

- **French:** Slice a loaf of French bread in half lengthwise. Spread with Peppercorn Rosemary Butter. Wrap in foil. Grill on direct medium heat for about 15 minutes until heated through.
- **Ciabatta:** Cut a loaf of ciabatta or sourdough into 1 inch (2.5 cm) thick slices. Brush both sides with olive oil. Grill on direct medium-low heat for 1 to 2 minutes per side until browned. Spread immediately with mashed roasted garlic. Sprinkle with salt and pepper, or spread with a flavoured butter.
- **Pitas:** Grill Greek-style flat breads on direct medium heat for 1 to 2 minutes per side until warmed through. Brush with Smoked Paprika Butter or your choice of flavoured butter.

VEGETABLES

- **Lettuce:** Cut small heads of romaine lettuce in half lengthwise through stem. Brush all sides with olive oil. Grill on direct medium-high heat until charred along edges. Serve whole with a drizzle of balsamic vinegar or your favourite vinaigrette; or, chop and make into a salad.
- **Corncobs:** Grill corncobs on direct medium-high heat for about 15 minutes until charred and blistered in places. Brush with Smoky Cranberry Butter or your choice of flavoured butter.
- **Vegetable Medley:** Cut a variety of vegetables such as zucchini, eggplant and mushrooms into similar-sized pieces. Toss with melted Curry Butter. Grill on direct medium heat until tender and browned. Brush with more Curry Butter if desired.

POTATOES

- **Baby Fans:** Thinly slice baby potatoes crosswise without cutting through bottom. Put in foil pan. Brush over and between slices with melted Chipotle Butter. Sprinkle with salt and pepper. Cover and seal with foil. Grill on direct medium heat for about 30 minutes until tender.
- **Sweet Potato Packets:** Put 1 lb. (454 g) of thinly sliced, peeled orange-fleshed sweet potato on a sheet of heavy duty or double-layered foil. Drizzle with olive oil. Sprinkle with 1 tsp. (5 mL) of chili powder, and 1/2 tsp. (2 mL) each of cinnamon and grated orange zest. Sprinkle with salt and pepper. Seal packet. Grill on direct medium heat for 10 minutes per side until tender.
- **Blue-Stuffed Potatoes:** Scoop out pulp from 4 medium, cooked potatoes. Mash pulp and combine with 1/2 cup (125 mL) cottage cheese, 2 to 3 tbsp. (30 – 50 mL) Blue Cheese Butter and 1/2 tsp. (2 mL) salt. Fill potatoes and grill on direct medium heat for 20 to 25 minutes until heated through.

FRUIT
Great with chicken, pork or seafood.

- **Pineapple:** Grill pineapple slices on direct medium-high heat for 2 to 3 minutes per side, brushing with sweet hot mustard or melted Curry Butter, until dark grill marks appear.
- **Peach:** Grill pitted peach halves on direct medium heat for 2 to 3 minutes until dark grill marks appear. Top with little pats of Smoked Paprika Butter or Rosemary Peppercorn Butter.

- **Mango:** Score crosshatch pattern into mango halves. Rub with jerk seasoning paste and sprinkle with brown sugar and ground allspice. Grill on direct medium-high heat for 1 to 2 minutes until dark grill marks appear.
- **Apple:** Combine equal amounts of butter and maple syrup. Add firm, tart apple wedges and toss. Grill on direct medium heat for 2 to 3 minutes until grill marks appear.

POLENTA
Use prepared polenta roll for convenience.

- Grill 1/2 inch (12 mm) thick slices of polenta on direct medium heat for about 5 minutes per side until heated through and grill marks appear. Top with pats of Blue Cheese Butter or spread with basil pesto.
- Grill 1/2 inch (12 mm) thick slices of polenta on direct medium heat for about 5 minutes per side until grill marks appear. Sprinkle with grated fontina cheese and grill for 1 to 2 minutes more until melted. Spoon prepared bruschetta on top.
- Grill 1/2 inch (12 mm) thick slices of polenta on direct medium heat for about 5 minutes per side until grill marks appear. Spread with olive tapenade and sprinkle with chopped fresh basil.

Glossary

arugula ~ known by many names, this salad green is slightly bitter with a peppery mustard flavour. It is often used in Italian cooking. You may find it in your grocery store or produce market sold as Italian cress, rocket, roquette, rugula or rucola.

basmati rice ~ this long-grain variety of rice has been grown in the Himalayas for thousands of years. Literally translated, *basmati* means "queen of fragrance." This name is particularly appropriate since basmati rice is known for its nutty flavour and aroma, which comes from the aging process used to reduce the moisture content in the grains.

bocconcini ~ small, round pieces of fresh mozzarella. Bocconcini are often sold packed in whey or water.

bulgur ~ sometimes known as bulgur wheat or burghul, this nutritious grain is widely used in Middle Eastern cooking and is similar to cracked wheat. Bulgur comes from wheat kernels that have been steamed, dried and crushed. Bulgur is available in coarse, medium and fine grinds.

chai ~ aromatic and spicy, this tea blend has been around for centuries in India. Tea leaves are blended with ground spices, often cardamom, cinnamon, cloves, ginger, nutmeg and pepper, for a distinctive flavour and aroma. You'll find chai available in your grocery store in liquid concentrates, powders, loose tea leaves and pre-packaged tea bags.

chili oil ~ this spicy, red-coloured oil is simply vegetable oil that's been infused with hot red chilis. The chilis infuse the oil with spicy heat and give the oil its characteristic red colour. Chili oil is widely used in Asian cooking.

chinese five-spice powder ~ a popular spice blend, used extensively in some Chinese cooking. This fragrant mixture gets its distinctive flavour from a combination of five different spices, usually cinnamon, cloves, fennel seed, star anise and Szechuan peppercorns.

cloves ~ reddish-brown and nail-shaped, this popular spice is actually the dried, unopened flower bud of the tropical evergreen clove tree. The name comes from the Latin word *clavus*, which literally means nail. Cloves can be found whole or ground and go great with both sweet and savoury dishes. A little goes a long way.

coconut milk ~ often used in curries, coconut milk can be quite rich and is made by combining equal parts of coconut meat and water. This mixture is simmered until foamy, then the coconut meat is strained and discarded.

coriander ~ known both for its seeds and leaves, which surprisingly taste nothing alike. The seeds are the dried ripened fruit of the plant and the leaves, also known as cilantro, are dark green and lacy. The seeds are used in baking, curries and pickling or for beverages like mulled wines.

cumin ~ related to coriander seed, cumin is a dried fruit from a plant in the parsley family. Aromatic and nutty, this spice is commonly found in curries and chili powders.

fennel ~ with a mild licorice flavour, the celery-like stems of this plant have a sweeter and more delicate flavour than anise, another licorice-flavoured ingredient. The feathery green leaves can be eaten, but are generally used only as a garnish or for a last-minute flavour boost. Fennel seed is also used for cooking, both in savoury and sweet dishes.

hoisin sauce ~ occasionally referred to as Peking sauce, this sweet and spicy sauce is often found in Chinese cooking. Made from soybeans, garlic, chili peppers and spices, this sauce is generally quite thick and is often used as a table condiment or to add flavour to meat dishes or stir-fries.

macadamia nuts ~ native to Australia, the macadamia tree was originally grown only for ornamental purposes. Unshelled, macadamia nuts are golden brown with a buttery, rich and slightly sweet flavour. They are sold either roasted or raw, and generally shelled. Macadamia nuts work great in both savoury and sweet dishes.

mirin ~ a sweet wine, golden in colour and generally with a low alcohol content. This ingredient is often used in Japanese cooking to add sweetness and flavour. Mirin is also sometimes known as rice wine.

miso ~ also known as bean paste, miso is an important ingredient in Japanese cuisine. Miso is made from fermented soybeans. The consistency is usually similar to peanut butter and it is often available in a variety of flavours and colours. Generally, lighter colours of miso are good for more delicately flavoured dishes, while darker colours work well with bolder flavours.

olive oil ~ a flavourful and fragrant oil, often found in Mediterranean cooking. The flavour and colour of olive oil can vary depending upon growing region, crop condition and the process used to press or filter the oil. Generally, the deeper the colour of the oil, the more intense the flavour.

paneer ~ also known as panir, this fresh, unripened cheese is common in Indian cooking. Paneer is made from whole cow or buffalo milk, curdled with either lemon or lime juice and with the addition of whey. It is then pressed, which gives it a firm texture, similar to that of tofu. Paneer is often served diced and sautéed in dishes such as dal, a lentil curry. It is also used as a protein in many vegetarian dishes.

panini bread ~ this Italian bread is generally quite thin and is used for grilled sandwiches. Translated, panini is Italian for "small bread."

pine nuts ~ a high-fat variety of nut that comes from inside the cone of certain types of pine trees. The cones must first be heated before the pine nuts can be removed. This labour-intensive process accounts for the higher cost of this ingredient. Pine nuts—sometimes known as Indian nut, piñon, pignoli or pignolia—are grown in China, Italy, Mexico, North Africa and the southwestern United States.

ponzu ~ a sauce made from a mixture of soy sauce, lemon juice or rice vinegar, kombu (seaweed), dried bonito flakes and mirin or sake. A common ingredient in Japanese cooking, ponzu is generally used as a dipping sauce.

porcini mushrooms ~ earthy-flavoured and pale brown in colour, these wild mushrooms are also known as cèpes, boletes and steinpilze. You won't often find this variety of mushroom available fresh in North American supermarkets; however, dried porcinis are common and are easily hydrated in hot water.

prosciutto ~ translated from Italian, prosciutto quite simply means "ham." This type of ham is generally seasoned, salt-cured and dried. The meat is then pressed, which gives it a firm, dense texture.

salsa verde ~ generally a mixture of tomatillos, green chilies and cilantro, salsa verde literally means "green salsa."

sesame oil ~ there are two basic types of sesame oil. The lighter is good for a variety of applications from salad dressings to frying and has a nutty flavour. The darker variety is much stronger-tasting and is used mainly as a flavouring ingredient.

suey choy ~ also known as Chinese cabbage, suey choy is cylindrical and has light green-coloured leaves. It's similar in flavour to bok choy.

tahini ~ a thick paste made from ground sesame seeds. Tahini is a common ingredient in Middle Eastern cooking and is used to add flavour to such dishes as hummus and baba ghanoush.

tapenade ~ often served as a condiment, this thick paste is commonly a mixture of ripe olives, olive oil, lemon juice, capers, anchovies, seasonings and occasionally tuna. Tapenade hails from the Provence region of France.

tikka curry paste ~ this variety of curry paste includes coriander and ginger and works best with chicken or fish. As the Hindi word tikka literally means chunks of meat cooked on skewers, this rich and aromatic paste is generally used to add flavour to kabobs or skewers.

tomatillo ~ similar in appearance to green tomatoes, tomatillos are small and green with papery husks. Tomatillos are occasionally allowed to ripen until they are yellow, but are generally used while still green. Cooking enhances the slightly acidic flavour of this fruit and helps to soften its thick skin. The tomatillo is sometimes known as a Mexican green tomato or jamberry.

wasabi paste ~ also known as Japanese horseradish, this green-coloured condiment has a sharp and spicy flavour. Sushi and sashimi are commonly served with a mixture of wasabi paste and soy sauce. Wasabi is made from the root of a plant related to horseradish. Some Asian markets may carry fresh wasabi, but powdered is also available.

Measurement Tables

Throughout this book measurements are given in Conventional and Metric measure. To compensate for differences between the two measurements due to rounding, a full metric measure is not always used. The cup used is the standard 8 fluid ounce. Temperature is given in degrees Fahrenheit and Celsius. Baking pan measurements are in inches and centimetres as well as quarts and litres. An exact metric conversion is given below as well as the working equivalent (Metric Standard Measure).

Spoons		
Conventional Measure	Metric Exact Conversion Millilitre (mL)	Metric Standard Measure Millilitre (mL)
1/8 teaspoon (tsp.)	0.6 mL	0.5 mL
1/4 teaspoon (tsp.)	1.2 mL	1 mL
1/2 teaspoon (tsp.)	2.4 mL	2 mL
1 teaspoon (tsp.)	4.7 mL	5 mL
2 teaspoons (tsp.)	9.4 mL	10 mL
1 tablespoon (tbsp.)	14.2 mL	15 mL

Cups		
Conventional Measure	Metric Exact Conversion Millilitre (mL)	Metric Standard Measure Millilitre (mL)
1/4 cup (4 tbsp.)	56.8 mL	60 mL
1/3 cup (5 1/3 tbsp.)	75.6 mL	75 mL
1/2 cup (8 tbsp.)	113.7 mL	125 mL
2/3 cup (10 2/3 tbsp.)	151.2 mL	150 mL
3/4 cup (12 tbsp.)	170.5 mL	175 mL
1 cup (16 tbsp.)	227.3 mL	250 mL
4 1/2 cups	1022.9 mL	1000 mL (1 L)

Dry Measurements		
Conventional Measure Ounces (oz.)	Metric Exact Conversion Grams (g)	Metric Standard Measure Grams (g)
1 oz.	28.3 g	28 g
2 oz.	56.7 g	57 g
3 oz.	85.0 g	85 g
4 oz.	113.4 g	125 g
5 oz.	141.7 g	140 g
6 oz.	170.1 g	170 g
7 oz.	198.4 g	200 g
8 oz.	226.8 g	250 g
16 oz.	453.6 g	500 g
32 oz.	907.2 g	1000 g (1 kg)

Oven Temperatures			
Fahrenheit (°F)	Celsius (°C)	Fahrenheit (°F)	Celsius (°C)
175°	80°	350°	175°
200°	95°	375°	190°
225°	110°	400°	205°
250°	120°	425°	220°
275°	140°	450°	230°
300°	150°	475°	240°
325°	160°	500°	260°

Pans	
Conventional - Inches	Metric - Centimetres
8 x 8 inch	20 x 20 cm
9 x 9 inch	22 x 22 cm
9 x 13 inch	22 x 33 cm
10 x 15 inch	25 x 38 cm
11 x 17 inch	28 x 43 cm
8 x 2 inch round	20 x 5 cm
9 x 2 inch round	22 x 5 cm
10 x 4 1/2 inch tube	25 x 11 cm
8 x 4 x 3 inch loaf	20 x 10 x 7.5 cm
9 x 5 x 3 inch loaf	22 x 12.5 x 7.5 cm

Casseroles			
Canada & Britain		United States	
Standard Size Casserole	Exact Metric Measure	Standard Size Casserole	Exact Metric Measure
1 qt. (5 cups)	1.13 L	1 qt. (4 cups)	900 mL
1 1/2 qts. (7 1/2 cups)	1.69 L	1 1/2 qts. (6 cups)	1.35 L
2 qts. (10 cups)	2.25 L	2 qts. (8 cups)	1.8 L
2 1/2 qts. (12 1/2 cups)	2.81 L	2 1/2 qts. (10 cups)	2.25 L
3 qts. (15 cups)	3.38 L	3 qts. (12 cups)	2.7 L
4 qts. (20 cups)	4.5 L	4 qts. (16 cups)	3.6 L
5 qts. (25 cups)	5.63 L	5 qts. (20 cups)	4.5 L

Tip Index

Index